COYOTE

Fascinating Animal Facts for Kids

Dylanna Press

Copyright © 2020 by Dylanna Press
Author: Tyler Grady

All rights reserved. No part of this publication may be reproduced, stored in a retrieval system, or transmitted by any means, including electronic, mechanical, photocopying, or otherwise, without prior written permission of the publisher.

Although the publisher has taken all reasonable care in the preparation of this book, we make no warranty about the accuracy or completeness of its content and, to the maximum extent permitted, disclaim all liability arising from its use.

Trademarks: Dylanna Press is a registered trademark of Dylanna Publishing, Inc. and may not be used without written permission.

ISBN: 978-1647900816
Publisher: Dylanna Publishing, Inc.
First Edition: 2020
10 9 8 7 6 5 4 3 2 1

For information about special discounts for bulk purchases, please contact:

Dylanna Publishing, Inc.
www.dylannapublishing.com

Contents

Meet the Coyote 6
What Do Coyotes Look Like 9
Where Do Coyotes Live? 10
Talking Like a Coyote 13
Built to Survive 14
What's for Dinner 17
Hunting Skills 18
Growing Up Coyote 20
Day in the Life 22
Surviving Winter 25
Family and Social Life 26
How Long Do Coyotes Live? 29
Predators and Threats 30
Coyotes and Humans 33
The Future of Coyotes 34
Test Your Coyote Knowledge! 36
STEM Challenge: Think Like a Scientist! 37
Word Search 38
Glossary 39
Resources and References 40
Index 41

Meet the Coyote

Coyotes are clever, adaptable mammals found from the frozen Arctic of Alaska all the way south to Panama. They live in nearly every type of environment you can imagine—deserts where temperatures soar above 100°F (38°C), snowy mountains, thick forests, grassy prairies, and even big cities like Los Angeles and New York. While most wild animals struggle when humans change the landscape, coyotes have actually expanded their range, moving into areas where they never lived before.

Their scientific name is *Canis latrans*, which means "barking dog" in Latin—a perfect name for an animal famous for its vocalizations. Coyotes are part of the dog family (Canidae), making them relatives of wolves, foxes, jackals, and your pet dog at home. But unlike their larger wolf cousins who have lost much of their territory, coyotes have thrived.

For thousands of years, coyotes have appeared in Native American stories as clever tricksters. Today, they still inspire both wonder and conflict as they live closer to humans than ever before. Understanding these remarkable survivors helps us learn to share our changing world with wildlife.

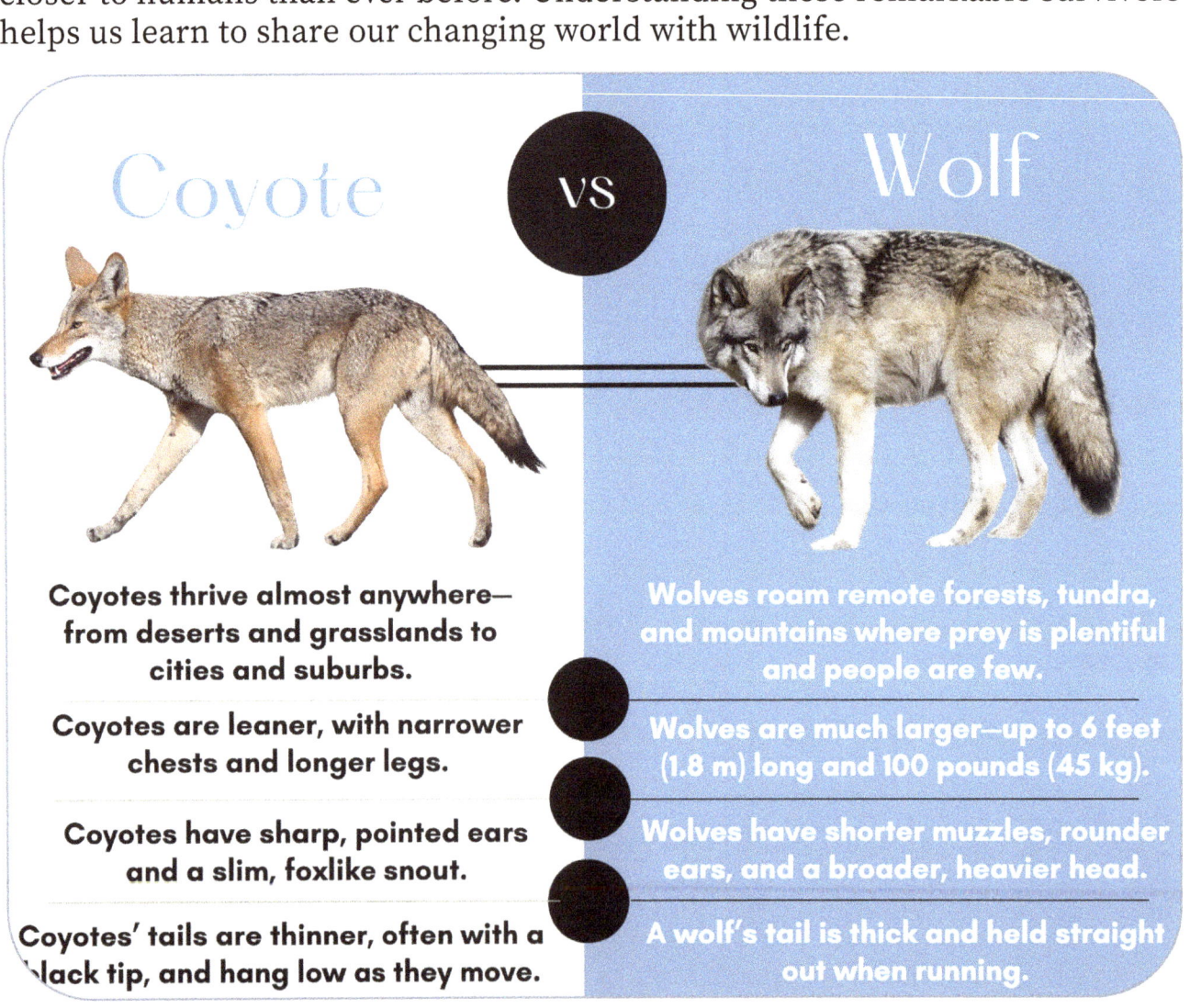

Coyote vs Wolf

- **Coyotes thrive almost anywhere—from deserts and grasslands to cities and suburbs.**
- **Coyotes are leaner, with narrower chests and longer legs.**
- **Coyotes have sharp, pointed ears and a slim, foxlike snout.**
- **Coyotes' tails are thinner, often with a black tip, and hang low as they move.**

- **Wolves roam remote forests, tundra, and mountains where prey is plentiful and people are few.**
- **Wolves are much larger—up to 6 feet (1.8 m) long and 100 pounds (45 kg).**
- **Wolves have shorter muzzles, rounder ears, and a broader, heavier head.**
- **A wolf's tail is thick and held straight out when running.**

Fun Fact: Coyotes are expanding their range every year and now live in nearly every U.S. state—even big cities like Chicago and Los Angeles!

What Do Coyotes Look Like

Coyotes are smaller than their wolf cousins but larger than foxes, weighing between 20-45 pounds (9-20 kg) and measuring approximately 32-37 inches (81-94 cm) in length. At the shoulder, they stand about 21-24 inches (53-61 cm) tall—roughly the size of a medium dog like a German shepherd.

Males are slightly larger than females. Both have lean, athletic bodies built for running long distances. Their bushy tails help them balance when making sharp turns while chasing prey.

One of their most striking features is their distinctive yellow or amber eyes that seem to glow in the dark. These keen eyes sit above a long, pointed snout packed with scent receptors that help them track prey and detect danger.

DID YOU KNOW?
You can tell a coyote from a dog by watching how it runs. Dogs hold their tails up when running, but coyotes always run with their tails down!

Their thick fur ranges in color from light gray to reddish-brown, often with darker fur along their backs and a lighter cream-colored belly. This coloring provides excellent **camouflage** in their varied habitats.

Where Do Coyotes Live?

Coyotes are true masters of adaptation, living in more diverse habitats than almost any other large North American mammal. Their range stretches from the northern reaches of Alaska and Canada south through the United States, Mexico, and into Central America as far as Panama.

Originally, coyotes lived mainly in the prairies and deserts of central North America. But over the past 200 years, as wolves were hunted and removed from much of their territory, coyotes expanded dramatically. Today they inhabit places their ancestors never reached—from Atlantic beaches to Pacific shores, from Arctic tundra to tropical forests.

Deserts and grasslands were the coyote's original home. Here they dig dens in sandy soil, hunt jackrabbits and ground squirrels, and survive extreme heat by resting during the hottest parts of the day.

Mountains and forests now house thriving coyote populations. They navigate steep terrain with ease, taking shelter in rocky outcrops or dense brush, hunting deer and smaller mammals among the trees.

Cities and suburbs have become unexpected coyote habitat. Coyotes now live in Los Angeles, Chicago, New York, and dozens of other cities. They den under highway overpasses, in parks, and even in suburban backyards. These urban coyotes have learned to navigate human spaces, hunting rats, rabbits, and occasionally raiding trash cans for food.

Wetlands and coastal areas also support coyote populations. They hunt waterfowl, fish, and small mammals near lakes, rivers, and marshes.

Unlike many animals that need one specific type of habitat to survive, coyotes succeed almost anywhere because of their flexible diet and behavior. From scorching Death Valley to frozen Alaska, from wilderness areas to city parks, coyotes have proven they can make a home almost anywhere.

Fun Fact: Coyotes raise and lower their pitch to make their pack sound larger and scarier to rivals.

Talking Like a Coyote

Coyotes are famous for their vocalizations and are one of the most "talkative" animals in North America. They use howls, barks, growls, yips, and whines to communicate with each other across their territory.

DID YOU KNOW?

Each coyote has a unique howl pattern, like a voice fingerprint.

Howling lets other pack members know where they are and helps coordinate hunting. Sometimes a lone coyote howls just to locate its family. At night, their distinctive yip-howls can carry for miles across open country.

Barking serves as an alarm call to signal danger or warn intruders to stay away from den sites where pups are hidden.

Growling between males is used to establish dominance and settle disputes without actual fighting.

The variety of sounds coyotes make is remarkable—scientists have identified at least 11 different vocalizations! Just two or three coyotes can sound like a dozen because they mix so many different sounds together.

Built to Survive

Coyotes have many physical adaptations that help them thrive in diverse environments from scorching deserts to frozen tundra.

Their **thick fur** provides insulation through cold winters and sheds in summer to keep them cool. The fur color varies by region—desert coyotes tend to be lighter, while forest coyotes are darker—providing natural camouflage wherever they live.

Their **bushy tails** aren't just for show. In cold weather, coyotes curl up and wrap their tails around their noses like a built-in scarf, keeping warm air close to their faces.

DID YOU KNOW?

Coyote ears work like radar dishes—each can turn independently to pinpoint sounds.

Sharp teeth and strong jaws let them catch and consume a wide variety of prey. Their canine teeth are designed for grabbing and holding struggling animals, while their back teeth can crack bones and grind tough food.

Long legs and powerful muscles make coyotes excellent runners. They can sprint at 40 mph (64 km/h) for short distances and trot at 25-30 mph (40-48 km/h) for miles without tiring. This endurance helps them patrol large territories and chase down prey.

Perhaps their greatest adaptation is their **intelligence and ability to learn**. Coyotes can solve problems, remember successful hunting strategies, and change their behavior based on experience.

Fun Fact: Their sense of smell is so strong they can detect prey hidden under a foot of snow.

COYOTE MATH

> 1. A coyote family of five hunts together. If each eats 2 pounds of food, how much food do they need in a day?
>
> 2. If a coyote eats 3 pounds of food a day, how much does it eat in one week?

A: 10 POUNDS; 21 POUNDS

What's for Dinner

Coyotes are **omnivores**, meaning they eat both meat and plants. This flexible diet is one of the secrets to their success—they can survive almost anywhere because they're not picky eaters.

The majority of their diet consists of meat. Small mammals make up their favorite meals: rabbits, mice, voles, ground squirrels, and rats. They also hunt larger prey when working in groups, occasionally taking down young deer or pronghorn antelope.

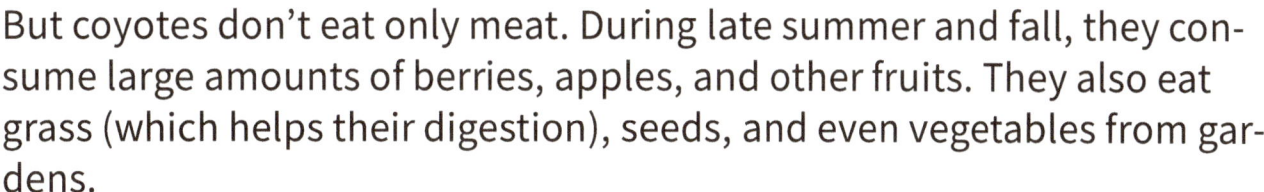

Coyotes are opportunistic feeders and will eat whatever is available. Their menu includes birds and eggs, fish, snakes, lizards, and insects like grasshoppers and beetles. In areas near humans, they sometimes prey on small pets such as cats and small dogs left outdoors.

But coyotes don't eat only meat. During late summer and fall, they consume large amounts of berries, apples, and other fruits. They also eat grass (which helps their digestion), seeds, and even vegetables from gardens.

Near cities, some coyotes have learned to **scavenge** from garbage cans and compost bins, finding discarded food that people throw away. This adaptability helps explain why coyote populations continue to grow even as other wild animals struggle.

Hunting Skills

Coyotes are skilled hunters with multiple strategies for catching **prey**. Their hunting style depends on what they're after and whether they're alone or with others.

When hunting small animals like mice or rabbits, a coyote typically stalks alone. It moves silently through grass or brush, using its excellent hearing to locate prey. When close enough, the coyote pounces with its front paws, pinning the animal down, then delivers a quick bite to the neck for a fast kill.

Coyotes can hear a mouse moving under a foot of snow! They use a technique called "mousing" where they leap high into the air and come down with their front paws on top of their hidden prey.

DID YOU KNOW?

Coyotes sometimes team up to hunt rabbits, taking turns chasing and ambushing.

When hunting larger animals like deer, coyotes work together as a pack. They use teamwork to chase and tire out their prey, taking turns running after it until the animal is exhausted. This cooperative hunting requires communication and planning.

Coyotes can run up to 40 mph (64 km/h) in short bursts and maintain speeds of 25-30 mph (40-48 km/h) for extended distances. This combination of speed, stamina, and cunning makes them formidable hunters.

They're also patient. Coyotes will watch and wait for the perfect moment to strike rather than wasting energy on chases they can't win. This intelligence helps them succeed where less careful predators fail.

Fun Fact: They can leap over 13 feet (4 m) in a single bound to catch prey.

Growing Up Coyote

Coyotes breed once a year, with mating season running from January through March. Pairs often mate for life, staying together for multiple years or even their entire lives.

After a pregnancy lasting about 60-63 days, mothers give birth between mid-March and April to litters of 3-12 pups, though 5-7 is most common. The number of pups often depends on food availability. When prey is abundant, mothers have larger litters.

Pups are born blind, deaf, and helpless, weighing less than a pound. Their eyes open after 11-12 days, revealing blue eyes that later change to the distinctive yellow-amber color of adults.

Both parents work together to raise the pups. The mother stays with the babies in the den, keeping them warm and nursing them. The father hunts and brings food back, **regurgitating** partially digested meat for both the mother and pups once they begin eating solid food.

As pups grow, they begin exploring outside the den around 3 weeks old. The parents teach them to hunt by bringing live prey for the pups to practice catching. By fall, at 6-9 months old, many young coyotes leave to find their own territories, though some stay with their parents through the first winter.

Day in the Life

Coyotes are primarily **nocturnal** hunters, most active during the hours between dusk and dawn. As darkness falls, a coyote begins its nightly routine—stretching, yawning, and setting out to patrol its territory and search for food.

The night belongs to coyotes. Under cover of darkness, they travel along familiar trails, stopping frequently to sniff the ground and air for signs of prey or other coyotes. They mark strategic spots with urine, leaving scent messages that say "I was here" to other coyotes who pass by.

A coyote might cover 10-15 miles (16-24 km) in a single night, trotting at a steady pace with occasional bursts of speed when chasing prey. Their keen night vision and exceptional hearing make them deadly efficient hunters in low light. The slightest rustle of a mouse in dry grass can trigger a lightning-fast pounce.

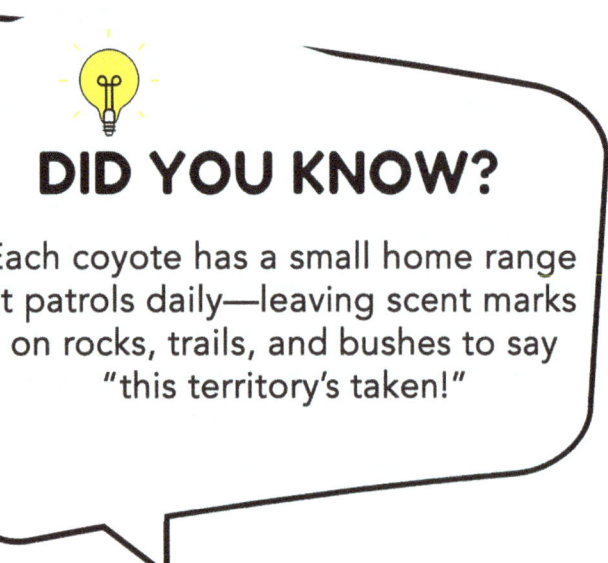

DID YOU KNOW?
Each coyote has a small home range it patrols daily—leaving scent marks on rocks, trails, and bushes to say "this territory's taken!"

In areas with heavy human activity, coyotes have become strictly nocturnal, waiting until people retreat indoors before venturing into neighborhoods and parks. But in wild areas, you might spot them during twilight hours—that magical time at dawn and dusk when many animals are active.

During the day, coyotes rest in **secluded** spots. Unlike wolves who use dens year-round, adult coyotes only den during pup-rearing season. The rest of the year, they sleep above ground in hidden places—curled up under thick brush, in tall grass, beneath rock ledges, or even in drainage pipes in urban areas.

Coyotes are light sleepers, often waking to watch and listen before settling back down. This alertness helps them stay safe and respond quickly to opportunities or threats. Even while resting, they remain aware of their surroundings, ready to spring into action at a moment's notice.

Fun Fact: Coyote families often meet up at sunrise to howl together before resting for the day.

Fun Fact: A coyote's winter coat can grow up to two inches thick, keeping it warm even when temperatures drop below −30°F (−34°C)!

Surviving Winter

Coyotes do not **hibernate** in winter. They remain active all year long, adapting to seasonal changes in weather and food availability.

They prepare for winter by building up body fat during summer and fall when food is plentiful. This extra fat provides insulation against cold and serves as an energy reserve when food becomes harder to find.

Their diet shifts dramatically with the seasons. In spring, summer, and fall, coyotes eat a varied diet of insects, berries, small rodents, and fruits. But in winter, many of these foods disappear. Insects vanish, plants die back, berries are gone, and even small mammals like mice become harder to catch under deep snow.

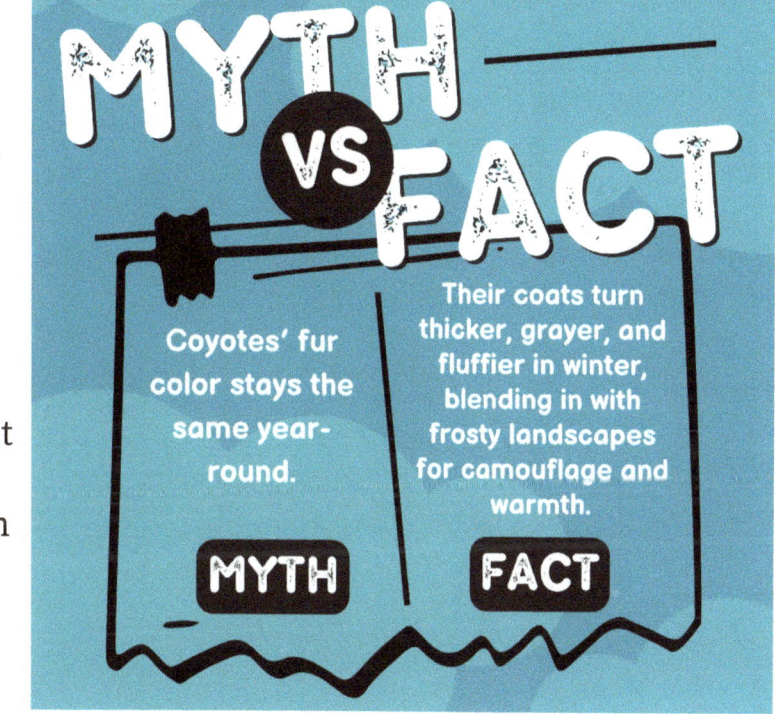

During harsh winters, coyotes increasingly turn to larger prey like deer. They hunt weak, old, or injured deer that struggle through deep snow. A single deer provides enough food for a pack to survive for several days.

Their thick winter coat makes a huge difference in survival. Starting in fall, coyotes grow a dense undercoat beneath their longer guard hairs. This double-layer coat traps air close to their body, providing excellent insulation. When temperatures plummet, coyotes can curl into tight balls, wrapping their bushy tails over their noses to conserve heat.

Winter is actually breeding season for coyotes, so despite the harsh conditions, this is when they focus on finding mates and establishing territories.

Family and Social Life

Coyotes are social animals with flexible living arrangements. They can live alone, in pairs, or in small family groups called packs, depending on territory and food availability.

A typical coyote pack consists of an **alpha** male and female pair along with a few of their offspring from previous years who haven't yet left to start their own families. Packs usually have 3-7 members, though sometimes just the breeding pair stays together.

The alpha pair leads the pack and are usually the only members that breed. They maintain a defined territory that the pack defends from other coyotes.

Territory sizes vary greatly—from as small as 2 square miles (5 square km) in areas with plentiful food to over 40 square miles (100 square km) in harsher environments.

Coyotes mark their territory boundaries with urine and feces, leaving scent messages that tell other coyotes "this area is taken." They also use howling to announce their presence and warn intruders to stay away.

Many coyotes live as **solitary** animals, especially young adults who have left their birth pack. These lone coyotes wander in search of unclaimed territory or opportunities to join a pack. Some eventually find mates and establish their own territories; others may remain solitary for life.

Pack members cooperate in hunting, raising pups, and defending territory, showing that coyotes form strong family bonds despite their reputation as loners.

Fun Fact: Coyotes have been observed playing! They chase each other, pounce on objects, and even play-fight, behaviors that strengthen family bonds and keep hunting skills sharp.

How Long Do Coyotes Live?

In the wild, coyotes typically live 10-14 years, though many die younger due to hunting, vehicle collisions, or diseases. In captivity, where they're protected from these threats, coyotes have been known to live up to 20 years.

The total coyote population across North America is estimated at several million individuals. Unlike many wild species, coyote numbers are not declining—in fact, their population continues to grow and expand into new areas each year.

Coyotes are classified as a species of "Least Concern" by conservation organizations, meaning they're not endangered or threatened. Their numbers remain healthy throughout their range, and in some areas, they're more abundant than ever.

This success is remarkable when compared to their larger cousin, the gray wolf. As wolf populations declined due to hunting and habitat loss over the past 200 years, coyotes expanded into areas where wolves once lived. Today, coyotes inhabit nearly all of North America from Alaska to Panama, while wolves remain only in isolated pockets.

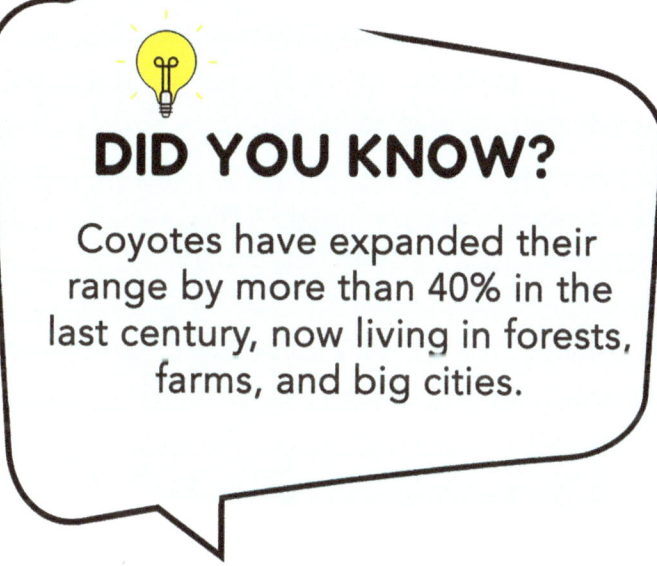

DID YOU KNOW? Coyotes have expanded their range by more than 40% in the last century, now living in forests, farms, and big cities.

However, despite healthy overall numbers, individual coyotes face significant **threats**. More than 400,000 coyotes are killed by humans each year through hunting, trapping, and government control programs designed to protect livestock.

Yet coyote populations remain **resilient**. When local populations decline, surviving coyotes often respond by having larger litters, and young coyotes from surrounding areas move in to fill the empty territories.

Predators and Threats

Coyotes have relatively few natural enemies because of their intelligence, speed, and adaptability. However, they are occasionally prey to larger **predators**.

Bears, particularly grizzly bears and black bears, will attack coyotes when they encounter them, especially near food sources. Bears are much larger and more powerful, making them dangerous opponents.

Mountain lions (also called cougars or pumas) sometimes hunt coyotes, particularly in western regions where their territories overlap. These big cats can take down prey much larger than themselves.

Wolves are perhaps the biggest threat to coyotes in areas where wolf populations still exist. Wolves view coyotes as competition for food and will kill them when given the chance. In fact, studies show that coyote populations are often smaller in areas with wolves.

Golden eagles occasionally prey on young or small coyotes, swooping down to grab them with their powerful talons.

Despite these predators, coyotes have thrived because they have few natural enemies and reproduce successfully. Their ability to adapt quickly has allowed them to spread widely across North America.

Predator vs. Prey: Who Wins the Chase?		
Predator	**Predator's Advantage**	**Coyote's Defense**
Wolf	Larger, stronger, and hunts in organized packs that can overpower a lone coyote.	Avoids wolf territory, hunts at different times, and uses superior agility to escape.
Mountain Lion	Silent and powerful ambush hunter capable of striking from cover or cliffs.	Detects danger early with excellent hearing and smell; flees before the cougar gets close.
Bear	Massive size and strength; will chase coyotes away from carcasses or food.	Gives up food and retreats quickly—speed and caution win over strength.
Golden Eagle	Attacks from above, targeting young or small coyotes.	Parents guard dens and pups stay hidden in brush or burrows when shadows pass overhead.

Fun Fact: Coyotes defend themselves by working together—parents distract predators while pups hide in burrows or brush.

Fun Fact: Coyotes have learned to look both ways before crossing roads and even use traffic lights!

Coyotes and Humans

The rapid increase in coyote populations has increasingly led to interactions between humans and coyotes as both species now share many of the same spaces.

Coyotes are naturally wary of humans and typically avoid them. However, they can become **habituated**—meaning they lose their fear—especially when people feed them either intentionally or by leaving food accessible. Fed coyotes become bolder and more likely to approach humans.

Despite growing human-coyote encounters, attacks on humans are extremely rare. Coyotes are far more afraid of us than we need to be of them. Most conflicts involve coyotes preying on pets or livestock, not threatening people.

The greatest threat to coyotes comes from humans. More than 400,000 coyotes are hunted and killed each year through various control programs. Ranchers and farmers often shoot or trap coyotes to protect livestock like sheep and calves. Many states have few restrictions on coyote hunting.

DID YOU KNOW? Coyotes play an important role in healthy ecosystems, helping plants, birds, and small mammals by controlling overpopulated prey species.

Vehicle collisions also kill thousands of coyotes annually as roads cut through their territories and urban areas expand into wild lands.

Yet despite this mortality, coyote populations continue growing because of their remarkable reproductive ability. When local populations decline, surviving coyotes compensate by having larger litters. Young coyotes from neighboring areas also move into territories where coyotes were removed, quickly refilling empty spaces.

The Future of Coyotes

Coyotes are remarkable and resilient animals. Through their intelligence and adaptability, they have not only survived but thrived in recent decades while many other wild species have declined.

Their success story is unusual in wildlife conservation. While most large predators have lost ground to human development, coyotes have expanded their range. They now live in ecosystems where they never existed before—from arctic tundra to tropical forests, from remote wilderness to the hearts of major cities.

What makes coyotes so successful? Their flexible diet means they can find food almost anywhere. Their intelligence lets them solve problems and learn from experience. Their speed and stamina help them hunt effectively. And their social flexibility allows them to live alone or in groups depending on what works best.

With their continued spread into urban and suburban areas, it is increasingly important that humans and coyotes learn to coexist peacefully. Understanding coyote behavior helps reduce conflicts. Simple steps like securing garbage, bringing pets inside at night, and not feeding coyotes can prevent most problems.

Coyotes play important ecological roles by controlling rodent populations, cleaning up carrion (dead animals), and dispersing seeds from the fruits they eat. They've become a permanent part of North American ecosystems.

Their resilience and adaptability make it likely that coyotes will continue to flourish in the years ahead, remaining one of nature's greatest survival success stories.

Test Your Coyote Knowledge!

Think you remember everything about these clever survivors? Test your knowledge and see how much you've learned about coyotes!

✏️ 1. What does the scientific name Canis latrans mean?
A) Running dog B) Barking dog C) Wild dog D) Smart dog

✏️ 2. How can you tell a coyote from a dog when they're running?
A) Coyotes run faster B) Coyotes run with their tails down C) Coyotes run with their tails up D) Coyotes hop instead of run

✏️ 3. What type of eater is a coyote?
A) Carnivore (only meat) B) Herbivore (only plants) C) Omnivore (both meat and plants) D) Insectivore (only insects)

✏️ 4. How fast can a coyote run?
A) 20 mph B) 30 mph C) 40 mph D) 50 mph

✏️ 5. When are coyotes most active?
A) During the day B) At night C) Only at dawn D) Only at dusk

✏️ 6. How many different vocalizations have scientists identified in coyotes?
A) 3 B) 5 C) 11 D) 20

✏️ 7. What is a group of coyotes called?
A) A herd B) A pack C) A pride D) A flock

✏️ 8. How long is a coyote's pregnancy?
A) 30 days B) 60-63 days C) 90 days D) 120 days

✏️ 9. Do coyotes hibernate in winter?
A) Yes, for 3 months B) Yes, but only in very cold areas C) No, they stay active all year D) Only the females hibernate

✏️ 10. What is the biggest threat to coyotes?
A) Bears B) Wolves C) Mountain lions D) Humans

Answer Key: 1-B, 2-B, 3-C, 4-C, 5-B, 6-C, 7-B, 8-B, 9-C, 10-D

STEM Challenge: Think Like a Scientist!

Want to learn more about coyotes through hands-on activities? Try these fun experiments and projects!

Coyote Communication Challenge

Topic: Science: Sound Wave Experiment
Coyotes use different vocalizations to communicate. Explore how sound travels!

You'll Need:
Empty paper towel tube; Plastic wrap; Rubber band; Rice or small beads; A partner

What to Do:

1. Stretch plastic wrap tightly over one end of the tube and secure with rubber band
2. Sprinkle rice on the plastic wrap
3. Hold the tube horizontally and have your partner speak, howl, or make sounds into the open end
4. Watch the rice bounce and dance with different sounds!

What You'll Learn:
Sound travels in waves that make the air vibrate. The rice shows these vibrations. Coyotes can hear frequencies humans can't, and their large ears capture sound waves efficiently!

Calculate Coyote Range

Topic: Math—Territory Mapping
Coyote territories vary from 2 to 40 square miles. Let's explore scale and area!

You'll Need:
Graph paper; Pencil; Ruler; Colored pencils

What to Do:

1. Let each square = 1 square mile
2. Draw a territory that's 2 square miles (could be 2×1 or arranged differently)
3. Draw a territory that's 10 square miles
4. Draw a territory that's 40 square miles
5. Compare the sizes!

What You'll Learn:
Area calculation, scale, division, and understanding how animals use space efficiently.

Word Search

```
Q Y P P N O I T A T P A D A M
S U R V I V A L B D E G V C A
S H J L T U H S T G N K O B M
A T L D S K L J A I C U C O M
E J A N P A A L T A N L A V A
N N E L M G F N P S I U L V L
N D V I K U U C O Y O T E S S
O H N I O H O M N I V O R E S
C A H M R P R E Y Q K J I B U
T W A O S O E C N A N I M O D
U C D X W B N T E I D R E B V
R L T L P L R M G N I N N U C
N N X V U R I E E C D F N X K
A I A X P V A N E N F B Z P X
L Z X R S G Y R G D T A S A O
```

ADAPTATION	DIET	OMNIVORES
ANIMALS	DOMINANCE	PACK
BREED	ENVIRONMENT	PREY
CAMOUFLAGE	HOWLING	PUPS
COYOTES	HUNTING	STALK
CUNNING	MAMMALS	SURVIVAL
DENS	NOCTURNAL	VOCAL

Glossary

adaptations – special features or behaviors that help a plant or animal survive in its environment

alpha – the highest-ranking animal in a group or pack

camouflage – coloring or patterns that help an animal blend in with its surroundings to hide from predators or prey

habitat – the natural home or environment where a plant or animal lives

habituated – to become used to something through repeated exposure

hibernate – when an animal spends the winter in a deep sleep to conserve energy

mammals – warm-blooded animals with hair or fur that give birth to live young and nurse their babies with milk

nocturnal – an animal that is most active at night

omnivore – an animal that eats both meat and plants

predators – animals that hunt other animals for food

prey – an animal that is hunted by another animal for food

regurgitate – to bring swallowed food back up to the mouth

resilient – able to recover quickly from difficulties; tough and adaptable

scarce – difficult to find; in short supply

secluded – sheltered, private, and hidden away

solitary – a lone animal that lives by itself

threat – something likely to cause damage or harm

vocalization – the sounds an animal makes to communicate

Resources and References

Want to learn more about coyotes and wildlife? Check out these trusted books, websites, and organizations that explore animal behavior, science, and conservation across North America.

Books

The Big Book of Animal Facts by National Geographic Kids — Discover amazing facts about coyotes and other wild animals.

Coyote: North America's Dog by Stephen R. Swinburne (Boyds Mills Press) — Beautiful photographs and fascinating facts about coyote behavior and survival.

Desert Night Shift: A Pack Rat Story by Conrad J. Storad (Arizona-Sonora Desert Museum Press) — Explore the desert ecosystem where coyotes hunt at night.

Predator vs. Prey series by Mary Meinking (Raintree) — Learn about predator-prey relationships including coyotes.

Websites

National Geographic Kids – Coyote Facts
kids.nationalgeographic.com/animals/coyote
Learn about coyote behavior, habitat, and fun facts with photos and videos.

The Humane Society – Living with Coyotes
humanesociety.org/resources/coyotes
Discover how to safely coexist with coyotes in your neighborhood.

Project Coyote
projectcoyote.org
Conservation organization dedicated to protecting coyotes and other carnivores through education.

National Wildlife Federation – Coyote Guide
nwf.org/Educational-Resources
Explore wildlife guides with information about coyotes and their habitats.

U.S. National Park Service – Urban Coyotes
nps.gov
Learn about coyote research in national parks and urban areas.

For Young Scientists

Urban Coyote Research Project – Chicago
urbancoyoteresearch.com
See real research on how coyotes adapt to city life with maps and data.

iNaturalist
inaturalist.org
Upload photos of wildlife you spot and help scientists track coyote populations.

Keep Exploring!

If you enjoyed learning about coyote, explore other titles in the *This Incredible Planet* series to discover more amazing animals—from sea turtles to penguins to elephants—and the habitats they call home.

INDEX

A
adaptations, 10, 14
alpha, 26
appearance, 9

B
barking, 13
bears, 30
breeding, 20

C
cities, 10

D
daily life, 22
deserts, 10
diet, 17, 25, 34
dogs, 9

E
ears, 14
ecosystems, 33, 34
environment, 6, 10
eyes, 9

F
forests, 10
fur, 9, 14, 24, 25

G
golden eagles, 30
grasslands, 10
growling, 13

H
habitat, 10
howling, 13, 26
humans, 33, 34
hunting, 18, 25

I
intelligence, 14, 34

L
lifespan, 29

M
mammals, 6
mating, 20
mountain lions, 30
mountains, 10

O
omnivores, 17

P
packs, 26
parenting, 20–21
population, 29, 33
predators, 30
prey, 17, 18, 25
pups, 20–21

R
range, 22, 29

S
size, 9
sleep, 22
smell, 15
social life, 26
speed, 14, 18, 34
suburbs, 10

T
tails, 9, 14
teeth, 14
territory, 26
threats, 29, 30, 33

V
vehicle collisions, 33
vocalizations, 13

W
wetlands, 10
winter, 25
wolves, 6, 29, 30

www.ingramcontent.com/pod-product-compliance
Lightning Source LLC
Chambersburg PA
CBHW040224040426
42333CB00051B/3434